THIS IS LOVE

An Expression of Non-Separation

Rebekah Maroon

This is Love: An Expression of Non-Separation

ACKNOWLEDGEMENTS

I bow my head to all parts of myself that have come before, with the burning desire for truth in their bones.

And to all those parts of myself that come after, with the same burning desire to find home.

INTRODUCTION

Welcome to this book. I am so pleased that this has happened.

This book is a collection of writings, interspersed with some poetry.

I hope the words found on these pages resonate so deeply that you are lost, and all that remains is resonance.

CONTENTS

CONTENTS CONTINUED

"Been looking for you everywhere...how beautiful that it was you who was looking."

PRETEXT

If life is going well for you...as in, you're having success in your relationships, in your work, etc...then there will probably not be much interest in this book or in this subject.

That doesn't mean, however, that if your life *is* going well for you that this message couldn't be heard, as there are no prerequisites or obstructions from this change happening.

But more often than not, when life isn't working for you, deeper questions begin to be sought and therefore, religion, spirituality, and philosophy are often turned to.

What is being spoken about here, as a possible answer to that discontent, is a change, a change from the human living through a mental story of itself, to the direct experience of life; without a dream someone living it. This could be called the end of human suffering.

Below, are some of the terms you may come across in this book:

Separate self ~ A phenomenon within humans where a mental identity has been energetically identified with, and makes the human feel incomplete and limited.

Time ~ An abstract idea which is purely mental, that humans have access to as a way to communicate.

To look in time ~ To imagine.

Seek ~ To have an idea in time of something you believe will complete you (make you feel whole) and for there to be energetic desperation to have it.

I

LOVE

This is a Love story from start to end. There may be pain at times and much sorrow, but always, always, this is Love.

Partaking in the journey of discovering who you ultimately are, is not a superficial journey; not a journey on which you take light snacks and a thin overcoat just in case it rains.

It is a journey in which you couldn't possibly understand or sufficiently prepare for.

It is a journey in which you think you are willfully choosing, but instead it is a current, wildly taking you along its rapids, meandering and bobbing along its still waters, and dropping down its waterfalls.

There's no hurry or rush. It's an endless dance.

When the investment and urgency of the destination lessens and lessens; when the grip of your fingernails on the side of the boat softens and softens; when your head and neck stops shooting forward to see if you're 'nearly there yet'... you will begin to sit back, start to breathe deeper, and see the beauty surrounding you.

You will see yourself; you will see that what was being looked for in time, is always here.

This, is Mystery.

This, is Love.

2

WHAT IS SUFFERING?

When the human body is born, it is fresh, it is

empty; pure looking-ness that remains like that always. What then happens is the brain begins to grow and language and memory develop. The abstracting ability of the brain strengthens; the ability to mentally imagine what's not there, to imagine what's not currently happening. This is the beginning of suffering. Not the ability to abstract or to imagine, that's a useful functioning for survival and for creativity; but the beginning of identification with thoughts and the imagined; as if thoughts and imagination are true reality. This is suffering - this ownership of thoughts and feelings, and the loss of your nakedness, your innocence. This is the start of seeking - to regain that which was felt to be lost. The loss of the natural coming and going of things, without ownership or investment; even the tears that may follow a loss, or the joy that may follow a gain.

3

LOST IN LOVE

I discovered that there was a possibility to go home.

So I put on my backpack with such excitement and glee. Finally, finally, there was a way out. I had no idea that the way out would be leading me in. Maybe if I'd known that, (and had the ability) I would have run a mile!

But gently, gently, without the mind even knowing, the outwards would be inwards, and the inwards would be outwards, and there would soon be no way of telling the difference.

4

WHO YOU ARE

Separation longs to find the lover, it longs to find

that which is permanent; that which will love it unconditionally, that which is stable. But the unconditional lover, that which is unchanging, can't be found by that which is changeable.

That which is permanent and unchanging, doesn't need to be found...how could it be lost?...If it is permanent and unchanging, how could it not be?

So, the dilemma only exists for the one that is changeable...the one that is not permanent, not stable...the seemingly separate one that is looking for the unchanging.

This is Love: An Expression of Non-Separation

Who. Are. You?

5

THIS IS ALL YOU

This sense of you being limited; this sense of you, belonging in a body, is just that - a sense - it isn't truth.

Why does your border stop at the edge of the body? Why does it not include the whole room and everything else that is appearing?! Because you've repeatedly been told that it doesn't...it's been believed, and *that* has become the experience.

This isn't an error. There's no one to blame. This seems to be the necessary way of the human. After all, we're not having a chair experience, or a curtain experience, we are having a human experience, so this human body is seemingly the reference point.

Now you are hearing that this is all you; every, little, single, thing -and not just the body.

Can this also be initially believed, repetitively heard and investigated, and this 'believed in border' be seen through? Can 'without border,' then become the experience? Who knows?! But 'without border' can only ever be right here, as this timeless moment, as this presence.

The bigger question then becomes, can border and no-border be at the same time?...This, I would say, is Love.

6

THE UNFINDABLE

There is something here that isn't something here; something that doesn't exist and yet is all existence.

It appears as every face, but its face cannot be seen.

It appears as every sensation, but it itself cannot be sensed.

It appears as every sound, but it itself cannot be heard.

It has no quality of its own, yet no quality can exist without it.

What is right here as everything, but cannot be held

onto?

What is this madness?!

What is it that is so unattainable by the mind, and yet still is?!

What a revelation!

7

DEATH

Death is here.

We long for death, as in the end of the suffering self, but as an apparent separate self, we also fear it.

"What will happen to me?" "What will happen to my story?" We cry...and yet, it's this very story we deeply wish to be free from.

Death happens every night as deep sleep. It's the end of this waking dream, the end of the appearances. There's nothing to be afraid of.

Death is always here, in every moment.

Now, there is death, offering rest.

Death allows everything to be. You can't have only one side of a coin; there must be death, there must be transformation, there must be silence for there to be music.

Life is inseparable from death.

Death is life, in disguise.

8

LONGING

What do you long for? What are you wanting?

If it's to be held until you disintegrate in my loving embrace...then there's no need to wait, you've got it!

9

NOTHING

CAN BREAK YOU

You may think and feel as if you are sitting here as a small being, an entity, encapsulated in that body.

If you would just relax a little, release your grasp and un-grip your fingernails from that location, then you would see the whole universe is yours.

10

THE MIND WON'T SAVE YOU

Thoughts...I wouldn't trust them.

Where are you going in the mind? What is the mind promising?

We trust the mind. We believe when we 'get there' in the mind, then we will bring our bodies along and then attend to them. It's always later: "I will be still later", "I will acknowledge and allow the not so pleasant feelings later."

The mind-train willingly keeps you busy with seemingly 'important' errands that are more important than the e-motion happening now.

This isn't to poo-poo the intellect, it's a useful tool; it's helped humans to evolve. Being able to imagine what could happen, what has happened, helps us to plan, communicate, and be creative.

Living in the intellect however, believing energetically that this mind-made self is you, setting up camp there...is suffering.

I Am Human

My heart was hurting yesterday...

I had to pull up at the side of the road twice,

to let it come up...

it was nice.

II

THE SCREEN IS ALWAYS

CLEAN

Just like the screen of an etch a sketch; no matter what you draw and write, the screen can always be shaken clean as if nothing ever happened.

For life to experience itself, scribbles and doodles are made. The etch-a-sketch isn't harmed in these drawings even when a scribble gets rubbed out. Was the scribble ever even there? "Yes," says the memory picture, "Huh...what scribble?" says the actual experience.

The doodle of pain, of gain, of loss, of anger, of laughter, of sadness, are the doodles of life, and just like in the toy etch-a-sketch, it doesn't need to be shaken to be cleaned, the screen is always clean regardless of what is currently being drawn.

That doesn't denote 'no action'; that doesn't mean you, as a human story/character become clean and still and holy. It means there's something that already is that, and the human story/character is a doodle being drawn.

12

NOWHERE ELSE

No-one's having a life 'out there'. You're not missing out.

Nobody exists 'out there' having more fun and getting more Love than you. You've been sold that idea. You've believed that idea. The mind uses that idea to compare its imagination of itself to its imagination of others.

It's all happening here.

"Love your neighbor as yourself"...but first you have to know yourself, and in so doing, you will immediately and intimately know your neighbour.

13

RELAXING BACK

INTO THIS

Awakening is a detoxifying process.

The relaxing back into this is the dying of the seeking energy that believes it will find some thing to feel whole.

The relaxing back into this reveals the pain, the trauma, the anger of abandonment, the seeking, the agitation; all that was being run away from by the seeker.

The relaxing back into this reveals the silence, the emptiness of being, the looker and experiencer of all that is - which is all that is!

The relaxing back into this isn't a personal endeavor,

something that you can do or can't do - it's something that happens.

When the relaxing is personally undertaken by the seeker as a means to an end, then there will be frustration and disappointment; that goal or that end will never be reached.

So, naturally there is a relaxation of the body that happens as this message of wholeness is energetically heard...how could there not be?!

14

CONTENTMENT

Contentment. What a wonderful thing.

To be at peace with life, to be at peace with what you are as this moment, to not be seeking in time for something else; but to be at home with this current expression, with this current circumstance, with this current condition.

...and for this to be enough.

15

WHEN TWO

BECOME NONE

All there is, is fullness of life.

All there is, is emptiness - that which doesn't exist.

When the mind that divides is dethroned and these seeming two are apparently bridged...then, there is true Love and completeness.

What more can be said?

16

DON'T TRY TO OWN THIS

Don't put your flag in the ground, be open to the endlessness of this; forget the idea of arriving.

Be like a demented shopper, pushing the trolley around the supermarket but with nothing inside.

Let the earth and scenery change constantly, like a homeless traveler on a train, with no final destination.

17

COMING BACK

When there is a collapse of living in a story of you, there is more of the bodily experience.

All the things that were being avoided by living in the mind, all the things that were being avoided by seeking in career, seeking in partners, seeking in spirituality - they all come up to be acknowledged.

There's no longer that removal from them. There's no longer that unconsciousness or denial of them because they are right slap-bang there, in the body; in the experience, appearing as this, and there's no one there to escape.

This might be painful being human, but that's because

you've been running from it for so long, because you thought you were small and would get broken by it.

Being human can be painful, but it can also be fun and exciting.

You wouldn't want to paint in just one colour, just like you wouldn't want to write a song with only one note.

Finding the ultimate nature of who you are, allows the coming back into the human, and its natural, harmonious, authentic way of being.

18

IT WON'T

DO IT FOR YOU

Until the discovery of yourself as Love.....this world will never be enough.

19

MYSTERY

I don't know what I'm talking about.

When you don't know what you're talking about...then we shall dance.

20

TRUST

Do not fight with yourself. Instead, melt into your heart.

Humble yourself to the one who touches your heart and not just your intellect.

If they truly speak of this, they will not try to keep you as a footstool but will *assist* and *insist* that you fly.

21

STRIPPED NAKED

Whenever you feel like you've got it, like you know what this is...

Let life humble you, and kick you off of your perch.

22

THIS IS LOVE

This, is what you've been looking for. This moment.

You believed it was in a destination, in an arrival, but destinations have disappointed you again and again.

This, life, simply and effortlessly happening. The sensation of bum on seat, feet on floor, the sounds, the sights, the thoughts, the feelings. This, is what is being spoken of and pointed to.

The is-ness of this happening; this is the mystery. There's nothing in time for you...there's nothing out there for you...there's nothing here for you.

This 'you' is a figment of the imagination, and it can only appear now, whispering sweet or not-so-sweet nothings about an imagined past and an imagined future, as an imagined self.

This, is it, with its sweet fragrance of Love.

23

GONE

These words, these squiggles on the page that your brain is interpreting into sounds, into meaning, are not true.

Don't take these words so seriously.

I don't know how else to say this.

Gone. Gone. Gone.

This is freedom.

24

PLAYING WITH MYSELF

How can I play without limitation?

How can I play without being something and then being an apparent other?

How can I know myself without losing myself to then find myself?

This is how I play.

Simply Myself

"I like what I like

and

I don't, what I don't."

25

HUMMINGBIRD

This isn't a message of hope or hopelessness, it's a song of freedom, with no intention...it just sings.

26

BEYOND YOURSELF

Let's imagine and say that this has been spoken about by thousands, if not millions, of humans for generations; a pointing to that which is beyond form.

It became known as God, Nirvana, or Heaven. And with this naming and concept of it, imaginings began of what it was like and how to get there and how you may look and behave once you arrived.

Methods and techniques were conjured up, steps to take to get closer, and signs to look for of your progress; such beautiful story-telling of the journey to beyond form.

But beyond form, has never been a place somewhere

else. It was never spoken of as a place to be found in the imagination, or as an object or an experience.

Beyond form is here, as form, as this room, as these hands, as these words, as everything that is appearing. These forms are not real and separate as they may sensorily appear to be. These forms are beyond form; they are no thing appearing as thing.

The seeker looks out in time, looks out in imagination, to find Heaven or Nirvana, when it can't be found because it was never lost; it is appearing as everything that is.

When it is seen that you are not something in existence; that you aren't some thing...then the body becomes free.

The healing and the unraveling of the human happens naturally, as part of this awakening.

What happens is a natural relaxing of the human and the traumas that are being held onto by the body. The patterns of the body may or may not disappear, but they relax and ease up, so whatever healing there is to be done can naturally happen; effortlessly, as life, without such importance and seriousness because this body and life no longer hold "*my*" freedom.

There is no end to the conditioning of the human, just like there's no end to life. This is an endless movement, an inhalation and exhalation of the universe.

No full stop is found in form.

No resting place is found in the story of this waking reality.

No "This is it," is found in the experience of human.

Hear this.

Home.

27

FOLLOWING THE LOVE

FLOW

It's a totally different way to experience life...to act

on and follow the bodily feeling or bodily knowing rather than to just live through the meaning and how things are "supposed" to be.

Acting from "yes", or what feels good rather than the confused-conditioned mind can seem reckless to the outside observer; but it's the most obvious, and most natural thing...to follow the flow and not the fear.

This also includes following the "no." The tendency is to have fear around letting people down or not going along with others, but listening to the "no" is also a very important aspect of our flow.

This isn't a personal separate doing where someone separate can follow or not follow it's flow...it's more of a pointing to the obvious. It's just what happens.

As the identification with mind decreases, the body can be heard. Your natural wants and preferences according to your nature, rather than the mind, are more easily known.

Why wouldn't there be a moving away from that which is painful? Why wouldn't there be a following of that which is pleasurable?...that would be such a natural movement, so what's standing in the way of that?

Look at the flower moving up towards the sun. Look at the mice choosing a reward over getting an electric shock; it's a natural movement.

We have been taught that life needs to be difficult and hard; that we need to sacrifice our joy and suffer. That pleasure is sinful and selfish, and only through sacrifice and hardship can we be happy. How absurd!

This is the idea that our 'cut off' society is based upon...reward will come in time, in the future.

Fear is activated and our power is taken. This keeps you in line and keeps you striving for the arrival; meanwhile, missing the joy and peace that is already here.

Missing life for the dream of after-life.

Rushing towards the flower shop...missing the scent from the flowers at the side of the road.

The Paradox

Standing still, not making a sound.
Oh, how we sang and danced.

28

OPEN YOUR ARMS

TO YOURSELF

There's nothing wrong with you, absolutely nothing.

Yes, you are not perfect as a human character, this is important to acknowledge, but you can't be a perfect person, that's just an idea. I say this because this is not a personal attainment; the human does not become perfect and then become enlightened.

The light of your true self is the perfection that shines through into the seeming world; this is what does the world good.

Yes, on some level you could say you could become more patient, more understanding, a little less selfish or whatever it may be, so be humble in that humanness, but don't listen to the mind, this is not a job to take on in the pursuit of happiness or enlightenment or of a better world. The layers of human conditioning are endless; the search for "what caused what?" ...you'll never find the start of!

If that character was all you were, then fair enough, endlessly fix away; but it's not the truth of the matter.

See the absolute beauty in yourself right as you are, in that character, that personality...and all that it's made up of. See how it couldn't have been any other way. See the perfection and the miracle in that this character or body-mind, appears at all!

See the perfection in the imperfection. There's nothing wrong with you that life didn't make so.

This is no thing or the Divine having this particular human experience.
Just like it's no thing or the Divine being every thing else.

29

NO THING

Let go of the finger pointing to the moon.

Let go of everything.

Let go of the meaning of these words...they'll do nothing for you.

"Yeah but, yeah but, yeah but...I can't let go, I don't know how."

Let go!

30

THE LOST CHILD

It's scary to grow up, to stand on your own, to not have an authority image standing over and above you.

Who will look after you?! What if you get it wrong?!

It's easier to stay small, to be a child. Then you can blame and point the finger if it goes wrong; then you can plead innocence in the event of prosecution on 'judgement day'; then you can wait, and not act, and let the world go by and not step up to play a part. It's like an obstruction to the flow of life, which is always changing, growing and expanding.

This is like the wonder and honesty of a child, but also the maturity and wisdom of an elder. This has nothing to do with a numerical age.

This 'stepping up' or 'growing up' I feel, is an act of human development. Literally, a growing up from child to adult. From limited to unlimited.

While you are playing as separate, you can only be a child wearing adults clothes, waiting and seeking for its lost constant parent, lashing out at those who have 'failed' to meet the part of this impossible role.

This isn't a human role. No one or no thing can be the 'mother' or 'father' that the separate sense of self so longs for.

Waking up from that dream of identification...this is seen.

Will You Love Me?

"I would abandon my flow
for the potential of Love.
I mistakenly believed
you were outside."

31

BOO

No thing or This is experiencing being human, just like no thing or this is experiencing being fox. Fox can't know being human, and human can't look through fox eyes and know being fox. So, in that way, it is alone in its manifested experience; it can't know another.

At the same time however, there is no other for it to know, it is all things. It is the human and the fox. It can't ever be alone.

Therefore the intimacy and closeness can't really be found in relationship with another. Relationship with seeming other can be beautiful and playful and encourage growth, compassion, and maturity, but it is always only with yourself...playing through another.

Therefore the only way to truly know another, is to truly know yourself.

The true intimacy and closeness that is longed for in another is in being, is in that which is animating everything; awakening unto itself as beyond form and yet as form...this is true intimacy...this is true Love.

32

SINKING

Sinking into this means there is a loss of everything; you lose.

You don't get to the finish line. You don't get to wear the crown. You don't get the adoration and applause; you fail.

This can be sad; to the mind and to the heart - this not making it. However, in this defeat, in this non-personal surrendering, in this exhaustion of trying...there is an opening - an opening to this boundless presence - a resting or a sinking back into this experience; into what is already here.

This is not a personal doing - something you can

believe, set your mind to, and then accomplish. This is something that is happening beyond this illusory idea of someone. This happens in spite of this dream-doer.

This is freedom beyond and without you. It is in no way personal. It doesn't belong to that idea of personal, therefore, how could this personal-idea-'you' ever arrive at it?

It's like when we were little children, before ideas and abstractions became strong. Before the ideas of ourselves, ideas of the world, ideas of others took hold, there was just full what is happening, without the removal of an I, or a witness of it.

This sinking back into this, is the removal of that I. Not a removal of thoughts, or mental knowing or the ability to describe or respond as a seeming character, but an end to that being contained within a border. An end to that being where you live. An end to that story-telling being reality. An end to the dream of separation.

It's Appearing

Be Happy!
Until that's no longer there,
then, be that!

33

STRIPPED NAKED AGAIN

Whenever you feel like you've got it, like you know

what this is...

let life humble you, and pull down your pants.

Humbled

        and

                Humbled

Again

        and

                Again.

34

REST AS YOURSELF

This already is everything you seek for. Not on a

so-called personal or human level. As a human, you want food, you want to do what you enjoy, you want connection with others, but those things are transitory needs and pleasures. These wants cause no problems in and of themselves, but they get hijacked by the seeker energy that believes it will get home through them. What is really longed for, is this; this emptiness which holds all form and yet, at the same time, *is* all form.

To believe home is in some form, is seeking; to seek for form believing it to be ever-lasting fulfillment, is torture.

This is Love: An Expression of Non-Separation

This, what is happening, already is what you seek.

Stop going out.

Rest as yourself.

35

NEVER IN WORDS

Language is simply sounds used to convey a message.

The tool of language is being utilized here to communicate, to describe something - to point beyond language.

This isn't a message spoken to teach the intellect something; this is not to be understood alone.

So, when the words, "Rest as yourself" are heard, not from the place of dream-independence, not from a place of learned information, but more as a poem - the beauty and simplicity deeply resonates.

Something has happened with this human brain. I vaguely have a memory of an experience where there had to be a letting go of the learned mental non-dual framework. There seemed to appear a choice between the effort of holding it up so that the mind could be intellectually right and follow a set teaching, or let it go and allow the heart to take over. Meaning, speaking from the heart, which required trust but didn't care so much about language and making logical sense. It just wanted to come out uninhibited.

This is how it is. Life wants to come out. Life wants to be free.

The body is being used.

This is the joy.

36

YOU ARE FREE

You are not in prison. You are not limited to a body.

You are not limited to an idea. You are not limited to a name, a colour, a nationality, a gender, a location, a condition, etc.

There is no border between what you are and what is appearing.

You are not in prison.

You are free.

37

A WAKING UP OF THAT

WHICH NEVER SLEPT

This is not an attainment of anything.

This 'waking up' is more of a removal of something. A removal of something that was seemingly in the way.

Something that was claiming to be independent. Something that was claiming to be experiencing. Something that seemed to be separately moving through something else.

This is a removal of the dream that a separate entity is living through a body.

It's a disappearance of a veil.

The disappearance of the veil, reveals that this is undivided.

Unbroken wholeness.

The emptiness of fullness and the fullness of emptiness.

It never slept.

38

IN THE TIGER'S MOUTH

Believing energetically that something is here for you...is seeking.

This feeling of incompleteness will lead the mind to search; causing untold stress, untold frustration, untold sorrow, anger, and disappointment.

This search will take you over field and farm, across cities and towns, over seas and mountains.

Looking for your lost one. Looking for your heart. Looking for your home. Looking for the arms of your lover.

You can never give up this quest.

Not until your head rests on its lap and you hear the unspoken words..."Home, Home...Home".

39

FINAL WORDS FROM THE AUTHOR

If I were asked, "What is Love?" or "What is God?" I would more than likely respond, "I don't know." This would be a true and honest answer.

However, I do know what Love or what God is...so deeply do I know what God or what Love is.

But I am unable to turn what Love or what God is into concepts and words to satisfactorily answer that question. That's how deeply I know what Love or what God is; I don't.

Don't take all this too seriously!

Chopping wood, fetching water, making dinner,

This is Love: An Expression of Non-Separation

reading a bedtime story; stepping out of time - this is seen.

What you look for is here:

The sound of the traffic.

The sensation of feet on floor.

The texture of the pages.

The glare of the light.

The chest opening and closing as the body breathes.

The mental picture - memories and projections.

The voice commenting.

The licking of the lips.

The readjustment and movement of the body.

This is Love: An Expression of Non-Separation

The shape of the room with its decoration and
content.

This is where I live.

This. This. This.

Printed in Poland
by Amazon Fulfillment
Poland Sp. z o.o., Wrocław